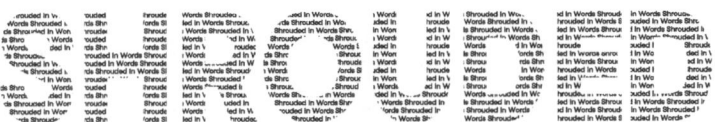

IN
WORDS

A Collection of Poetry

PATRICIA QAIYYIM

For more information, contact the author at patricia@patriciaqaiyyim.com.

First paperback edition December 2023

Book cover design and interior layout: Galan Graphix Graphic Design Services

ISBN 979-8-9871951-2-3 (paperback)
ISBN 979-8-9871951-3-0 (eBook)

Published by Patricia Qaiyyim
www.patriciaqaiyyim.com

Congress of Library Cataloging in Publication Data Control Number: 2023920430

Table of Contents

Dedication

To my parents, who gave me life
and a lifetime of love.

To my husband, whose love and
support always lifts me higher.

To my family, through your
presence in my life, you have all
shaped the person I have become.
And with your love and support, I
have the courage to be that person.

Acknowledgments

I want to acknowledge and thank God for His grace and blessing. I pray that He continues to guide me as I endeavor to inspire, motivate, and educate through thought-provoking works, written and spoken.

I want to thank my family and friends for their love, support, and encouragement as I worked on this project. Your words of encouragement and love, which I can never repay, continues to inspire me. I love you all!

To the literary professionals who have helped me make this book the best it could be. Your touches have added the polish that will allow this book to shine.

Community

"The greatness of a
community is most
accurately measured
by the compassionate
actions of its members."

Coretta Scott King

Power

Sometimes, the world likes to think
that only a few have power,
but we all have power, a power that
no one else can devour.

My power may not look like your
power, but that does not mean that I
have none,
or that my power can, in any way, be
undone.

I am not talking about monetary
power, physical power, or even
coercive power.
I am talking about a power that
shines in my darkest hour with the
strength of a tower.

You may have the power of the
oppressor,
but I have the power to not let you
make me feel that I am lesser.

You may have the power to block the
path and show me no grace,
but I have the power to focus and
find new ways to continue my race.

You may have power that others
readily recognize and respect,
but I have the power to work hard so
that my actions have the right effect.

You may have the power that some
envy and strive to obtain,
but I have the power that will last a
lifetime and help me sustain.

I am talking about the power that
resides within me, a gift for me alone,
a power that keeps me strong when
everything says I should feel defeated
and not able to stand on my own.

A power that gives me the strength
and the determination to stand tall
and be strong
when everything around me wants
me to believe that somehow I am all
wrong and that I don't belong.

My power may not be like your power,
but don't get it wrong,

I have the power of a lion, and I stand
strong and ready to fight to make
sure I belong.

For the Next Generation

What we say, we should say with honesty
and compassion.

Because what we say, good or bad, is our
message to the next generation.

What we do, we should do with integrity
and conviction.

Because what we do, good or bad, is our
legacy to the next generation.

What we create, we should create with
foresight and wisdom.

Because what we create, good or bad, will
be the tools for the next generation.

What we exhaust, we should exhaust with
much consideration and self-restraint.

Because what we exhaust, good or bad,
will be but a fable to the next generation.

What we leave behind, we should
leave behind with circumspect and
consideration.

Because what we leave behind, good or
bad, will be the foundation for the next
generation.

Tomorrow Will Be Better

Today, the sun came up
My feet were shackled
And they called me property
The sun set and I thought
Tomorrow will be better

Today, the sun came up
My back bore welts and my burden was heavy
And they called me slave
The sun set and I thought
Tomorrow will be better

Today, the sun came up
My rights were denied and my dignity stripped
And they called me Negro
The sun set and I thought
Tomorrow will be better

Today, the sun came up
I faced discrimination and fought racism
And they called me black
The sun set and I thought
Tomorrow will be better

Today, the sun came up.
I am fighting inequality and striving for a
better life
And they call me African American.
The sun sets and I rest
Because I know tomorrow will be better.

The Pandemic of Two Thousand and Twenty

In the early part of that year, it took the world by
storm. Not just a city or nation
but the whole world, without a thought or
hesitation.

Was it an act of God, a strange culling, or a cyclic
event like the 100-year flood?
No one knows for sure, and it really doesn't matter
once Covid has entered your blood.

It changed how we live, from how we learn to how
we work and even mourn for our dead.
And I sometimes wonder when it will come to a
head.

No one can say for certain, but I hope, and I pray...
that we will prevail at the end of the day.

We've lost millions to a death that seems senseless.
And it has left so many of us feeling defenseless.

When it has come and gone, how will we all be?
Some say changed forever.
Well, I pray changed for the better and stronger
than ever.

I know I am ready to, once again, live in a world
without masks, gloves, or a shield between us.

And ready for us to move forward and recount the
whole experience thus...
Something we survived once we learned to adjust.

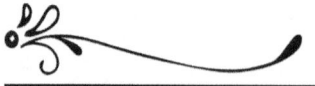

History or Truth?

All our lives, we study and explore to learn our history.
But whether that history is truth seems a bit of a
mystery?

It's long been said that history is written by the victor.
Do the victors record the truth, or does their self-
preservation act as a constrictor?

Do they write with an honesty that might offend
them?
Or with a little less morality so that we do not
condemn them?

Do they write with a truth that honors the conquered
as well as the victor?
Or a truth that allows them to claim every action a
necessary part of the big picture?

Are we capable of writing a history that is really the
truth?
A truth, without exception, that does not require a
sleuth.

What if we wrote a history that was completely true
and without omission?
Wouldn't we really learn the price of each victory and
its true definition?

They say if we do not learn from our history, we are
condemned to repeat it.
I say, if our "history" is not truth, we might learn a
lesson, but the lesson won't be legit?

Heartbroken but Hopeful

Heartbroken by the tragedy that fills the
headlines...
but hopeful that, in the end, the unity of our
nation will still shine.

Heartbroken that a mother, a family, a nation
mourns an avoidable death...
but hopeful that this loss, to change, will give new
breath.

Heartbroken that a few who have sworn to
uphold and protect have failed...
But hopeful that those more resolved to uphold
and protect will prevail.

Heartbroken that so many in our nation are
hurting and broken...
But hopeful that our nation will heal and change
won't be just a token.

Heartbroken that some would use this
opportunity to agitate, riot, and loot...
But hopeful that we won't be dissuaded from
what's really in dispute.

Heartbroken that some people of our nation
won't see beyond the effect...
But hopeful that we will move to unite, support,
protect, and respect.

Heartbroken that for such injustice, we seem to
have tolerance...
But hopeful that it will become another practice
of our past rather than a continued occurrence.

Heartbroken that so many of us must warn our
sons and daughters that they could be a target
simply because of the color of their skin...
But hopeful that telling their sons and daughters
is a conversation our children won't have to begin.

A Woman... And A Vice President... All in One

If you asked the average citizen who was vice
president in the decades past,
Most can't recall from elections gone by. I can't
even recall the one before last.

But this year is different, a monumental event
where, before only men could stand.
Now, there's a woman in this great nation elected
as second-in-command.

In one of the most powerful nations, today stands
one woman beside one man.
Elected together, and together, they'll stand to
represent our nation and its plan.

Some have said, "It is almost a crime," while others
cried out, "It is certainly about time."
A glass ceiling now shattered to shards, and
shining through is Kamala, in all her sublime.

She is counted among a few as a US VP; she
stands, in fact, as one of only forty-nine.
And we all stand with her, ready to see her shine.

This woman... so poised, so strong, so smart.
Standing on her own merit, right from the start.

Inspire

Let your life be one that inspires...

Inspire someone to be bold.

Bold enough to step out on faith.

To believe in themselves when no one else does.

To move out of their comfort zone in order to be better people.

Inspire someone to chase their dreams.

The dream that seems impossible, that no one else can see, that may require much, that will not be suppressed.

Inspire someone to say, "It's time to start."

Time to start, even when others say you're too young, even when others say you're too old, even when you don't know quite how to start.

Inspire someone to break the cycle that brings them harm.

Break the cycle for themselves and for future generations so that the hurt and harm come to an end.

Inspire someone...period.

What If?

What if every man and every woman decided to make our world the best it can be?

What if we really treated everyone with respect?

What if the color of our skin really didn't matter?

What if every woman carried the same worth as every man?

What if every child had enough to eat and a place to call home?

What if everyone said what they meant and meant what they said?

What if "for the people" was truly for every person?

What if we didn't need laws to tell us how to behave and more importantly how to treat others?

What if all of our leaders led with everyone in mind?

What if all our neighbors were truly neighborly?

What if our faith wasn't a reason to judge us without knowing us?

What if we take our responsibilities as seriously as we take our own lives?

What if everyone felt safe in their everyday life?

What if our character was more important than our monetary worth?

What if you and I decide to move from "what if" to "I will"?

II
Family

"Call it a clan, call it a
network, call it a tribe,
call it a family: Whatever
you call it, whoever you
are, you need one."

Jane Howard

Family...More Than Genetics

I don't need shared genetics to tell me who I am, and I don't need genetics to tell me who you are to me.

I don't need a shared DNA to know that you are as much a part of me as the color of my eyes or the texture of my hair.

I don't need a shared bloodline to feel the love you have shown me, remember the lessons you have taught me, or feel a sense of comfort that comes when I hear your voice.

I don't need a shared ancestry to know that my life and my future will be linked to you through the contributions you have made in my life.

I don't need a shared reflection to see so much of you in me...from how we have the same walk, accent, and small nuances that come from a lifetime of living in the same house and sharing the same family.

No, I don't need genetics to tell me that you are my family and that I am your family. I only need the love we share, the sense of belonging you give me, and the simple fact that I love you... and that family is more than genetics.

A Mother's Love

Through birth, you gave me life.

Through your touch, you gave me love.

Through your smile, you gave me joy.

Through your words, you gave me wisdom.

Through your limits, you gave me discipline.

Through your success, you gave me hope.

Through your tears, you gave me strength.

And every day, I am blessed to have you as my mother.

If I Had One More Day with You

If I had one more day with you, we could sit and do nothing or do whatever needs to be done.

I would tell you how much I miss you. Or how often I think about you, wishing I could tell you just one more thing. Like stories of your grandchildren and their children, your legacy.

If I had one more day with you, I wouldn't waste it thinking about the 'what ifs' or 'why nots'.

I would spend it reminiscing about all the times we had together...how you made me laugh, made me feel safe and loved...remembering all the times I was happy just to be with you.

If I had one more day with you, I would treasure every second, knowing there would be no more days with you.

I would love to have one more day with you, but I would gladly take one more hour with you.

If I had one more hour with you, I would tell you how much I love you, how much I miss you, and how much of you I see…in my memories and the faces of your grandchildren.

I would tell you how much you mean to me, how you made me believe in myself, and that anything was possible if I worked for it.

If I had one more hour, I would tell you how much of who I am is because of who you were, how through your legacy, you are gone but still living on.

I would love to have one more hour with you but would settle for one more minute with you.

And if I had one more minute with you, I would simply enjoy your presence and your smile for that one more minute. I would kiss your cheek one more time and tell you that I love you and how blessed I am to have had you as my dad.

My Sister, My Friend

A sister loves you because you are family.
A friend loves you because you are you.

A sister shares your childhood memories.
A friend shares in creating new memories.

A sister respects your individuality.
A friend accepts your individuality.

A sister will support you through the
good and bad times.
A friend will go with you through the
good and bad times.

A sister treats you like a friend.
A friend treats you like a sister.

What a blessing to have you as both my
sister and my friend.

How I See You

As a child, I saw you as my mom, nothing more
and nothing less, because that is what I needed
you to be.

As a teen, I saw you as my provider, disciplinarian,
and even sometimes as my enemy because that
is what you needed to be to help me become my
best me.

As a young woman, I finally saw you as a woman,
with flaws, dreams, successes, and failures, which
helped me to see that life is full of ups and
downs, successes and failures.

As a mother myself, I saw you as my role model
and mentor, guiding me along my journey because
I needed your guidance and support to help me
be the best mom I could be.

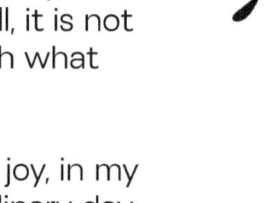

In the end, I saw you in all your frailty, but more
importantly, I saw you at your strongest, living
and striving to endure what life brought to you
because I needed to know that, above all, it is not
what life brings you but how to deal with what
life brings you.

These days, in my quiet moments, in my joy, in my
sorrow, and even in the middle of an ordinary day,
I miss you as my mom, nothing more and nothing
less because that is the you that I miss the most.

The Loss of My Brother

You are my brother, and I have always known you.
When I needed you, you were always there,
coming around as if on cue.

I have not a single memory of my early life
without you.
You and I are the same, like two colors of a slightly
different hue.

Every single day of every single year growing up,
you were always there.
Sometimes my partner-in-crime; sometimes a
bother, but always letting me know you care.

As we grew older, we took different paths, moving
in our own direction.
Sometimes near and sometimes far, but even so,
we've always had a special connection.

We seemed to pick up right where we left off
when life brought us together again.
We'd catch up like no time had passed; it was
easy with you. I never had to pretend.

Looking back, we weathered some storms; some
we caused, and some life brought to us.
At times, our strength was tested, but we always
persevered and considered each other a plus.

And then, in a second, you were gone...still my
brother, but no longer around.
Your absence is like a missing limb. The loss of you
in my life is so profound.

And now, I have experienced life without you,
some days, I miss you deeply.
But my memories keep me company when I feel
the loss so completely.

My Mother and The Woman You Are

As a child, I never thought of you as anything other than my mother. I didn't see the woman that you were, shaped by a life that you lived before I became me.

A life of a young child who lost the very thing that you needed...your mother. And lived a life without your father, whom maybe you felt just couldn't bother.

A child living a life in a world where you sometimes felt alone...living life and wondering, where do I belong?

As a child, forced to grow up before your childhood was done. The trust of childhood gone, your body abused, and your soul a little bit bruised.

A young woman, with all you had experienced, you were willing to do all you could to feel the comfort and safety that comes with a relationship built on love and trust, two things that you had not yet experienced to its' fullest.

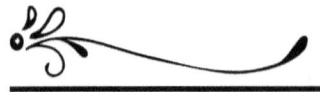

A life filled with ups and downs, heartache, and pain that resulted in your looking for love and becoming a mother; maybe before you were ready, but still a mother, like so many others.

A woman, no, a mother making decisions for yourself and your children, sometimes for your sake and sometimes for theirs, so they wouldn't have to carry the burden of guilt.

As a mother, you tackled life with all you had and made a way when there seemed to be no way for you and your children to get ahead.

A mother who made sacrifices beyond belief just so your children would feel the love you didn't always feel as a child. And maybe, just maybe, you got some of it wrong, not out of malice but out of loving the only way you knew in your effort to belong.

And decades later, here I stand, looking at you not just as my mother but as the woman you are, in all the beauty and pain that is your life...and as a woman who became my mother when I became me, despite all her strife.

My Perfectly Imperfect Father

When I was a young child, you were perfect, it seemed.
So strong and so smart...you could do it all, whatever you dreamed.

Never once did I question your love for me.
Because that love, like you, was perfect, you see.

And when I was with you, I knew, without question,
that I, too, could do anything if I had the notion.

As I grew older, I realized that you were not quite perfect, to a small degree.
But even with this, you were still perfect for me.

And your love was still perfect and gave me the strength I needed to help me see.
That in this world, the perfection of love is the secret...the key.

As a young woman, I could quite clearly see the truth of your flaws.
Your imperfections were clear and, maybe for a moment, gave me pause.

And I could see that you could not do everything,
but who among us can?
But I could also see that you would do everything
you could for our clan.

And just as clearly, I could see that greater than
your flaws were the strength of your love.
And that love was helping me to see...that you
don't have to be perfect...only willing to love.

As a woman, I now see that no one is perfect; we
all have our faults.
But that is no reason for our love or lives to come
to a halt.

And I hope that for every little girl, the perfection
of love blurs the imperfections of her father, at
least for a while.
So that she can see the perfection and the
strength of his love in her world so that she can
withstand any trial.

III

Love

"Love is something eternal,
the aspect may change,
but not the essence."

Vincent Van Gogh

You Are... My Love

Your eyes are the mirror that reflects all
that is good within me.

Your smile is the sun that brightens my day.

Your kiss is the spark that ignites a fire
within me.

Your arms are the source of my warmth
and comfort.

Your strength is my strength when the
feeling of defeat is within me.

Your love is the essence that fills a void.

Your very presence is the nourishment that
feeds the soul within me.

You are and always will be...my love.

My Valentine

Today is Valentine's Day...
the day our nation chooses to celebrate love.

As I reflect on you, me, and the love that we
share...
I realize that all the things in the world, to
my love, could never compare.

As I reflect on the life that we have
together...
I realize that nothing we face could cause us
to untether.

As I reflect on this day and the things I could
give...
I realize that nothing I can give is comparable
to the life that we live.

As I reflect on this holiday, it's just like any
other day...
I realize that I choose this day and every day
to celebrate our love in every possible way.

The Sea of Life

As we sail on the Sea of Life,
I take comfort in knowing that we sail together.

I know there will be times when storm winds
blow, the waves swell, and our boat will feel like it
is at its breaking point.

I know there will be times when turbulent winds
and gale forces will blow us off course, and we
will have to struggle to stay on the course we
have set.

I know there will be times when your desire to
go west will clash with my desire to go east and
create storms as great and strong as any tsunami.

I know that these times will pass, and we will
emerge stronger. I know that as we face each
storm, each struggle, each clash, we will forge
ourselves into an even stronger team.

I know that together, we will enjoy each sunrise
and sunset and bask in each day that the wind
fills our sails and calmly moves us further along
the sea of life and closer together.

And I also know that as long as you are with me,
we will sustain...and life will be good.

If

If I could only go to one place...I would go where you are.

If I could only be one thing...I would be the love of your life.

If I could only have one thing...I would have you by my side.

If I could only have one passion...I would have the passion of our love.

If I could only say one thing...I would say "I love you" from the depths of my soul.

If I could only have one wish...I would wish you a lifetime of happiness.

If I could only be thankful for one thing...I would be thankful that you are a part of my life.

Because of You

Because of You, our children know love...
love that is unconditional and everlasting.

Because of you, our children know discipline...
discipline that shapes their presence and is the
foundation of their future.

Because of you, our children know honor...
honor that comes from being a man in the world.

Because of you, our children know family...
family and what it means to be a family.

Because of you, our children know determination...
determination that will help them achieve their
dreams.

Because of you, our children know laughter...
laughter that comes from deep within and
spreads joy to all who hear it.

Because of you, our children know music...
music and what it adds to life.

Because of you, our children know the love of
their father.

From There to Here

From there, where we began the journey that
is our life as husband and wife.
To here, where our journey includes a life
filled with love for one another and hope for
our future.

From there, where we were two people on
their way to becoming us.
To here, where we are one...one pair
intertwined into one couple, one family, one
that was two, now linked through love and
commitment.

From there, where we could only imagine our
life together.
To here, where I cannot imagine my life
without you.

From there, where we thought our love could
weather any storm that would come our way.
To here, where we know our love will endure
whatever life brings us.

From there, where all those years ago, we
promised to love, honor, cherish, and obey.
To here, where all these years later, I'd do it all
over again.

IV Parenthood

"There are only two
lasting bequests we
can hope to give our
children. One of these is
roots, the other, wings."

Johann Wolfgang von Goethe

My Child

On an ordinary day, an extraordinary thing happened. I learned that inside of me, your life had begun.

At times, I would often sit and marvel at the miracle that would be my child.

At times, I was scared just thinking about the awesome responsibility that comes with being a mother; even so, I was always overcome with joy at the very thought of you.

As you grew inside me, stronger each day, so grew my love, which words could not convey.

With every move and kick I felt came wonder and amazement that, inside of me, my child was growing.

Finally, you arrived so strong, healthy, and beautiful. My joy was no longer containable. I laughed, I cried, and I knew that I would love you unconditionally.

I looked in your face, and I saw your father, I saw myself, and I saw the love that we have for one another and our hope for the future.

Even now, each time I look at you, I know I have a purpose and a reason...and that reason is you.

My Children

You are all different and individual, yet all the same in that you are the children of your parents.

It has been my honor and privilege to be your mother; each of you is a blessing and a gift from God.

It is my wish and my hope that you continue to support and love one another as you move forward with life and all that it brings.

It is my prayer that God continues to keep you and bless you and guide you through all that you face.

As you make your way in the world, remember what you should hold on to most are the people, and not the things, in your life.

No matter where I am or where you are, you should know that I love you more than words could ever express.

And in your future, as in your past, I am your mother, and my love for you will last as long as the sun rises every morning and sets every night.

You Are My Grandchild, My Lovebug

You are my lovebug.
I love your smooth caramel-colored skin, so lovely and kissed by the sun.

You are my lovebug.
I love the twinkle in your beautiful brown eyes that sparkle when you laugh.

You are my lovebug.
I love the tight curls of your hair and the way it surrounds your head like a magnificent crown.

You are my lovebug.
I love watching you grow and blossom into the beautiful person you are becoming.

You are my lovebug.
I love thinking about your future, and where it will take you, I can only imagine.

You are my lovebug.
I love that you reflect the generations before you and provide a glimpse of the future generations.

You are my lovebug.
I love that you are my lovebug.

The Struggle for Independence

When you were one, you wanted to walk alone, but
I needed to hold your hand...
and I felt your struggle for independence.

When you were two, you wanted to do it your way,
but I needed you to do it mine...
and I felt your struggle for independence.

When you were five, you wanted to go by yourself,
but I needed to follow...
and I felt your struggle for independence.

When you were eight, you wanted your own
housekey, but I needed to lock the door...
and I felt your struggle for independence.

When you were twelve, you wanted your freedom,
but I needed to set limitations...
and I felt your struggle for independence.

When you were fifteen, you wanted to make the
decisions, but I needed to make them...
and I felt your struggle for independence.

Yesterday, today, and tomorrow, you will struggle
for independence, and I will struggle to protect you.

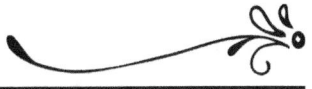

Into Manhood

As my beloved boy enters manhood, I see...

His world is growing, like a Redwood, upward and to heights unseen.

His love is expanding, like moss on a tree, encompassing all it touches.

His excellence is surging forth like a tidal wave, strong and unstoppable.

His worth shines through like the sunlight peeking through the clouds after an abated thunderstorm.

His confidence is rising, like the temperature on a hot summer day in the middle of the desert.

As my beloved boy enters manhood, I see his childhood left behind like a forgotten toy...
and I see him standing tall, ready to forge his way in the world like the majestic man he is destined to be.

Into Womanhood

As my beloved girl enters womanhood, I see...

Her world growing, like the mighty oak, upward and out.

Her love expanding, like a vine, covering all that it touches.

Her excellence erupting forth, like the fire of a volcano,
magnificent and unstoppable

Her beauty shining, like a rose glistening with morning dew.

Her confidence rising, like the river after an overdue thunderstorm.

As my beloved girl enters womanhood, I see her girlhood left behind like a butterfly's cocoon...
...and I see her emerging like a butterfly bursting from that cocoon.

Twenty-One Life Lessons

Life is not always fair, but our Creator is, and His love is everlasting, His blessings countless, and His strength enough to carry you through.

Your parents love you not because of what you are but because of who you are...their child, and that won't change.

Measure your success not by what you have accomplished but by the happiness you have and the happiness you bring to others.

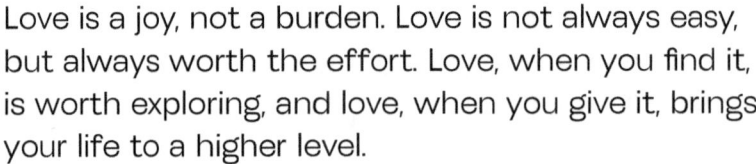

Love is a joy, not a burden. Love is not always easy, but always worth the effort. Love, when you find it, is worth exploring, and love, when you give it, brings your life to a higher level.

In life, you should depend on hard work to get ahead rather than sheer luck. Most of us are not that lucky.

You are smart, intelligent, and talented. All great traits, but to keep them and enable them to grow, you must use them.

For many in life, beauty is only skin-deep, and after a while, it begins to fade. In you, I see the beauty of your reflection and the beauty of your soul; both are magnificent.

As a member of the human race, you owe it to yourself and all mankind to love your neighbor. Never look down on anyone, and when you can, lift someone other than yourself.

Family is a gift from God, and you are a gift from God to your family. Love your family and let them love you.

A good marriage takes hard work, sacrifice, dedication, faith, and love. A good marriage gives you a strong partnership, a friend, a shoulder to lean on, someone to laugh with and grow old with.

Money is necessary for many things in life, but it is not necessary to laugh with a friend, love your family, to take joy in simple things like sunshine, a summer rain, or the beauty of a butterfly.

You are a gift and should treasure yourself as a most precious gift. Whether it be your friendship, body, mind, or love, you should give of yourself with great care and consideration.

Don't take others for granted. Always appreciate all that you have and all that you are.
We all get angry, but when you learn to let go of the anger, you will have more room for joy and love.

Continued

Forgiveness does not come easily, but it is necessary to move beyond the pain and hurt that sometimes comes in life.

A true friend stands by you, will not let you down, and will not let you lie to yourself. If you want a true friend, you must be a true friend.

Honesty is the best policy; be honest with your family, friends, boss, and employees, but most importantly, be honest with yourself and don't compromise your honesty for anyone.

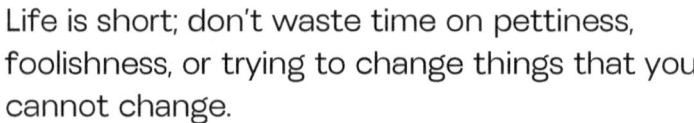

Life is short; don't waste time on pettiness, foolishness, or trying to change things that you cannot change.

Life is short. Live it to the fullest, take chances, see the world, and always strive for happiness.

You must believe in yourself and your abilities if you expect others to believe in either or both.

Know that you can always count on Mom and Dad, but we are only here for as long as God's plan allows, but He is there for you forever...always remember that.

Stepparent

A stepparent becomes a parent through love, the blending of families, and all that it entails.
Taking what was two, making it one, forging a path that leads to a new trail.

They commit to love not just their spouse but their spouses' brood.
Working to establish a home that is welcoming and not the basis for a feud.

They work not to replace but to complement what already prevails.
To be parent to one or many, with their new family, they hope not to fail.

They may face what seems to them like an uphill trod.
Working hard to get from a child just the tiniest but telling nod.

They offer strength and security, a bond built on love, not blood.
A bond that, with time, will blossom much like a flower from a tiny bud.

They stand ready and willing to step in to do what needs to be done.
To provide and to love, without question, their new daughter or son.

They will give their time and resources to one not of their own seed.
To help raise, impart love, and share wisdom to help the next generation succeed.

As Your Mother

As your mother, I marveled at the miracle of your birth, and I marvel at the person you have become.

As your mother, I would move Heaven and Earth to ensure you are okay.

As your mother, I have freely given all I have so that you can be all you can be.

As your mother, I want nothing more for you than for you to be healthy, happy, and productive.

As your mother, I can think of nothing you can ever do or say to change my love for you.

As your mother, I have watched you struggle and succeed, fall and get back up, and take on life with such enthusiasm.

As your mother, I have watched you grow
and thrive, and I have rejoiced in every
accomplishment.

As your mother, I have felt every pain you endured,
every joy you have felt, and watched you grow
through every experience.

As your mother, I will stand by you, support you,
and always love you.

As your mother, I am proud to call you my child,
and I hope you feel the same.

As your mother, letting go was so hard, but
watching you stand alone is amazing.

As your mother, I will laugh with you, cry with you,
and always be with you...even when you cannot
see me.

V
Faith

"Faith is not something
to grasp, it is a state
to grow into."

Mahatma Gandhi

Thank You

Thank you for the Word that I find in the Bible.
For now, it is the teachings that I share with my
children.

Thank you for the sacrifice that you made on the
cross.
For now, it is the way for me to enter the
Kingdom.

Thank you for the love you have shown me, even
when I didn't love myself.
For now, it is the love that I share with others.

Thank you for the joy that lives in my soul.
For now, it is the joy that endures all things.

Thank you for the tribulations that have resided in
my life.
For now, they are the patience that I will always
possess.

Thank you for the many blessings you've
bestowed upon me.
For now, they are the hope that, every day,
sustains me.

Thank you for the sorrows I have had to endure.
For now, they are the source of my strength at
my core.

Thank you for bearing the burdens that I could
not bear myself.
For now, they remind me of my faith that helps
me go on.

Thank you for the glory that you bring to me.
For now, it is the light that shines for others to
see.

Thank you, Dear God, for being you...
and for loving me.

Loss

Loss is painful and unavoidable. As we live, we experience loss.

Loss can be simple, like the loss of a job, a car, a house, or other material things.

Loss can be immeasurable, like the loss of a spouse, a parent, a sibling, a child, an unborn child, a friend, or even a beloved pet.

Loss can also be the loss of what was not. Things dreamed of, hoped for, prayed for, but never manifested.

Loss...is inevitable in life. Because we live, we are bound to experience loss; the two seem to be intertwined.

And because we are only here for a short time, our very own end will come...and that will be a loss to those we leave behind.

While loss is painful and unavoidable, loss (and the ache of loss) is softened by the love of God.

The love of God brings comfort in the very midst of loss. A comfort that allows us to breathe...just when we cannot fathom taking one more breath.

The love of God brings peace in the very midst of loss. A peace that comes just when we think there can be no peace...a peace that surpasses our very understanding.

The love of God brings quietness in the very midst of loss. A quietness that quells the noise of life and loss...just when it becomes almost unbearable.

So, while loss is painful and unavoidable, there is a love that can comfort and support us as we endure the painful and the unavoidable.

That love is the love of God, and all we need to do is go to Him, lean on Him, and let His love be what we cannot be...strong and steadfast in the very midst of loss.

The Strength of My Faith

My faith allows me to step out when I can't see the way.
To trust that, by faith, I will be where I am supposed to
be at the end of the day.

My faith sustains me like nothing else can.
Allowing me to hold on and endure no matter what the
demand.

My faith protects my soul when I feel lost and alone.
Allowing me to feel safe because I know that I am never
really on my own.

My faith holds me up when my burdens make me feel
like I cannot stand.
Allowing me to hold on until I can, once again, take
command.

My faith gives me hope when I should feel rejected.
Allowing me to wait with patience because I know I am
protected.

My faith strengthens me in my darkest hour.
Allowing me to depend on its immeasurable power.

My faith lifts me up from my deepest despair.
Allowing me to rise and stand up when others might not
dare.

When I am at my lowest, heavy with sorrow, burdened,
and feeling like I have no power...
I hold fast to my faith because it gives me hope for a
brighter tomorrow.

When I Look Around

When I look around, I cannot help but wonder at the result
of your infinite ability.
To know that you alone created the universe in all its infinity.

You created it all...from nothing to something. With a word,
you created Heaven and Earth.
Like an artist with the stroke of a paintbrush, to the world
and all it contains, you gave birth.

To create a world that supports humanity and all under its
dominion.
Bringing purpose and order to what was chaos in every
dimension.

You created the Earth, the winds, waters, and soil, creating a
world that only you can rule.
And I am amazed at what you have provided for humankind,
with only your Word as a tool.

You created mankind, breathing life into dust to create
woman and man.
To create us in Your image was a part of your majestic and
magnificent plan.

When all seemed lost, Your love demanded we be given a
second chance.
And your Son gave His life for my life; in His death, for me,
He took a stance.

I cannot see you nor touch you, but I feel your infinite
presence in every way.
And for as long as I breathe, I'll give you thanks and praise
every day.

I Have Learned

I have learned that I can see God in the
quiet moments and in the chaos of it all.

I have learned that I can find God not only
in the church but in the beauty of the world
wherever I look.

I have learned that God is in the big things,
in the little things, and in the in-between
things.

I have learned that God can be seen
everywhere, in everything, and in everyone.

I have learned that I can communicate with
God in my own way and with my own voice.

I have learned that to hear God, I must be
willing to be open to Him.

I have learned that God will wait for me to
come to Him and welcome me when I do.

I have learned that my relationship with
God is dynamic, always growing, ebbing, and
flowing.

I have learned that God is the source of me
and the world, and all is the creation of God.

State of Mind VI

"You don't have to be positive all the time. It's perfectly okay to feel sad, angry, annoyed, frustrated, scared and anxious. Having feelings doesn't make you a negative person. It makes you human."

Lori Deschene

Adoption... Because I Love You

I think of you often and the decisions I made.
In all this time, not even a little, did my love for you fade.

A decision to let someone else be the parent that I simply could not.
A decision to live without you, one that left my stomach in knots.

In my life without you, there are a lot of decisions that I have often questioned.
But giving you up so that you'd have a better life was a decision that I never, for a minute, regretted.

Every day, I miss having the chance to get to know you or to watch you grow.
But, in my mind, I have watched you grow and talked to you often since the day I let you go.

I love you today just as I have loved you from the day you were born.
And a life without you has always left me feeling slightly torn.

Today, as I reflect on my decision and its impact, not just on me but on you and the family you gained.
I hope and pray that it has left you with more love and joy that, with me alone, you may have never attained.

I carry you with me, deep in my soul, because without that little piece of you, I could never be whole.

In The Dark of Night

"Gripped by panic" and "frozen in fear."
Just cliches in the morning light but very real in
the dark of night.

The anxiety comes from a source unknown.
Waking me quickly, leaving me breathless and
feeling alone.

The apprehension I feel is inescapable and real.
The words to describe it; I cannot find but my
deepest fears, it does reveal.

Fears...some unknown and some unspeakable.
Invading my brain when I least expect it, and I feel
disjointed and a bit unstable.

In the morning light, my fears are at bay.
The anxiety was pushed aside but never really far
away.

It only takes a thought to bring it all back into sight.
To plunge me, alone, into the anxiety that comes in
the dark of night.

In the Quiet Moments

In the quiet moments, I can find the peace and calm that escapes me in the hustle and bustle of the day.

In the quiet moments, I can revel in the silence and listen to my thoughts without the interruptions of life getting in the way.

In the quiet moments, I can tune into myself and find the simple joys of just being me.

In the quiet moments, I can let the pains and sorrows of the day wash away.

Sometimes, life can get so busy and so loud that the quiet moments seem to elude me when all I want are those quiet moments.

Today, there seems to be more to do, more to see, and more to hear.
And the more time it takes to "do more" seems to leave me less time to revel in the quiet moments.

In the quiet moments, I can sit, listen to my thoughts, and reflect on my life's joys and blessings.

Today, I want to leave it all behind and sit in the silence that seems so hard to find.
If only for a little while, I want to be alone and listen to my thoughts.

Taking more time to get to know myself and giving less time to all the hustle and bustle of the world.

Tuning out all the noises of today...and tuning into all that is within me.

Turning off the phone and the things that take up so much of my time.
And turning to my thoughts, letting them lead me where they will.

Reveling in my own company and loving my own company in the quiet moments.

Just Keep Breathing

When your life gets hectic, and you feel like you
don't know up from down...
and even though you are not in water, you feel like
you are about to drown.

As you struggle to make sense of it all, and you
don't know what to do...just keep breathing.

When your soul is wounded, and your mind has
gone numb from the pain...
and you're wondering just how much longer or
how much more you can contain.

As you struggle to find the strength to go one step
further...just keep breathing.

When your hope is gone, and you feel so much
alone...
and you feel more ache and loneliness than you
have ever known.

As you struggle and wonder if you even want to go on...just keep breathing.

When you look around and can't seem to find your reason or purpose...
and you feel like the world might be better if you were not on the Earth's surface.

As you struggle to hold on and not let the darkness take over...just keep breathing.

And when the day comes that you decide to get the help you need...
...you realize that with a little help, from the pain, you can be freed.

As you no longer struggle to take that next step, you realize all you needed to do was just keep breathing.

The Silence Between Us

The silence between us is a silence that has become so
loud.
Almost deafening and, at times, covering me like a shroud.

The words are within me. I hear them, sounding as loud as
a shout.
But no matter how I try, they never seem to make their
way out.

The silence between us is like a chasm almost too wide to
cross.
Always leaving me sad and lonely and feeling at a loss.

At times, I try to reach out with the words that I feel.
But they seem trapped inside my head, as if it were a trap
made of steel.

The silence between us runs wide and so deep, like the
sea with its untold depth.
Constantly leaving me ragged and feeling like I can't
catch my breath.

Sometimes, I sit and try to remember all the words that I
can no longer voice.

But bringing them out to share with you no longer seems like a choice.

The silence between us has become an almost constant companion.
Making the distance between us feel as big as the Grand Canyon.

I wonder if you feel the silence that sits between us; if, like me, you are ready to break its bond.
But instead sit there wondering if you did speak out, would I even respond.

The silence between us is growing, becoming even bigger than us.
Leaving us so far apart that I begin to wondor if it's worth all the fuss.

But imagine if we refuse to let the silence consume our lives and our world.
And once again become lovers who talk, letting each and every word unfurl.

Until finally, the silence between us is gone, the words within no longer deferred,
so that every single syllable we want to speak is finally heard.

The End of Us

The time has come to say goodbye...goodbye to our marriage and our life together.

As we part ways, there are so many things that I find myself reflecting on, and I can't help but feel a sense of sadness, a sense of loss, a sense of failure, and even a sense of fear of not knowing how to move forward without you. And, as I reflect, I can't help but mourn the loss of our life together.

As I mourn the loss, I am overwhelmed with the memories of our life story. Our celebrations, our children, and all the moments that brought me so much joy. But also, all the breakdowns over the years that have brought us to this point. Not one big thing but a thousand little things, that we ignored, and they have added up and fell on us like a ton of bricks.

So, now I must move forward alone...for myself and my peace. As I move forward, the sadness of our loss mingles with the hope of my new beginning.

A beginning that I must take alone on a path to my new life. A life without you and without the comfort that comes from being together for so many years.

As we both face the coming days, months, and years, I hope we both find a new life, a new joy, and a new sense of wonder that somehow fills the void that we both now face. And maybe even a new happiness that matches the joy we once had as husband and wife.

So now...we move forward, no longer a couple but two people on new paths with a shared history, if not a shared future.

The Darkness

It began as a single thought, deep inside, where
the darkness prevails and has become more of me
than even I am.

It nudges me awake as the day begins, gently
invading my body and mind, where it will stay
throughout the day.

It is my ever-present companion, constantly in my
thoughts and my body.

It is with me always, a constant barrier between
me and everything else.

It clings to me all day long, not for one moment
releasing me from its powerful grip.

It invades my mind, disrupting my concentration,
lest I forget its presence.

It consoles me when nothing else will and hurts
me like nothing else can.

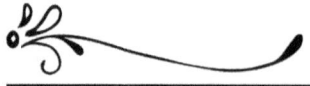

It feeds itself on what was my happiness, leaving only sadness and despair in its place.

It laughs when I cry, growing stronger as my pain grows while I become weaker.

It has become a way of life for me, consuming all thoughts and ready to ignite.

It is there at the end of the day, holding me as I succumb to the weariness that it brings.

It is there when I close my eyes at night, gently caressing me as I pray for sleep and peace.

It is there when he reaches out to me, quietly slipping itself between him and I.

It squeals with joy when I vow that I will no longer be its prisoner, for it knows that now, it is more of me than I am.

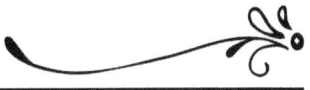

Sometimes

Sometimes, it is all I can do to get out of bed --
struggling to get up when all I want to do is lie
down.

Sometimes, just taking a shower is exhausting -- the
energy leaves my body like water down the drain.

Sometimes, just a smile is all I can manage --
anything more, even a "hello," might bring on a flood
of tears.

Sometimes, the screams in my head are so loud I
can't hear myself think -- not able to listen or focus,
lest the screams escape my head for all to hear.

Sometimes, the only thing I want is numbness -- for
just a while, to not feel the pain and sadness that
invades my brain.

Sometimes, I just want to curl up and sleep -- but
my mind will not shut down, keeping me awake as
the minutes and hours tick by.

Sometimes, I am amazed that I can stand in front
of others and converse -- always wondering if they
can see behind the mask that is my smile.

And sometimes, when I least expect it, I can see
a glimmer of joy, a spark of hope -- making all the
other "sometimes" a little less painful and me a little
more hopeful.

VII

Reflection

"By three methods we may learn wisdom: First, by reflection, which is noblest; Second, by imitation, which is easiest; and third by experience, which is the bitterest."

Confucius

A Reflection on Beauty

If you look, you can see that beauty comes in many forms, but only if we refuse to be tied to one concept of beauty norms.

If you look, you can see that, in life, there is much beauty to be found. This beauty can be seen if we just look around.

If you look, you can see the beauty in the wrinkles, representing a long-lived life, filled with insight and wisdom.

If you look, you can see the beauty in the scars that tell a story of pain, followed by healing. Pain and recovery that might have had some of us reeling.

If you look, you can see the beauty in what makes one different. The beauty of being different, standing strong, and even defiant.

If you look, you can see the beauty that resides in one's soul, a beauty that brings forth the kindness of words, a ready smile, a helping hand, or a gentleness that can help others feel whole.

If you look, you can see the beauty in our world. But only if we are free from the constraints of having only one concept of beauty and instead let all the beauty of the world freely unfurl.

Life is Too Short

Life is too short to long for what could have been...
...and too short not to cherish all that you have.

Life is too short to dwell on the things you cannot change...
...and too short not to celebrate all the changes we have made.

Life is too short to worry about what tomorrow holds...
...and too short not to focus on what today offers.

Life is too short to cry about the love you've lost...
...and too short not to take joy in the love you have.

Life is too short to wait for dreams to come true...
...and too short not to pursue your dreams.

Life is too short to wallow in sadness and self-pity
...and too short not to seek happiness and fulfillment.

Life is too short...live it to its fullest.

Life Is A Journey

Life is a journey that starts with a single breath in just one second,
in that moment, on the day you are born.

While so many journeys all seem the same,
after a while, your journey becomes uniquely yours to claim.

Each day on your journey is a chance...a chance to do something worthy and good,
to leave your mark, and not worry if you are misunderstood.

To walk your path with honesty and a sense of pride that won't be denied,
 is a choice, a decision, that only you can decide.

Don't let others decide the choices you make or the direction you take,
because these choices are ones you must make for your very own sake.

Each day on your journey will bring something new.
Something to discover and explore as you make your way through.

The people you meet may walk on your journey for a long time or just a short while,

Maybe only for as long as they bring you joy and companionship, making you smile.

Some people you meet may choose not to walk your path; your journey may not be for them,
but don't let their decision bring you sadness or cause you to condemn.

And some may walk for a very short time, leaving before you or they are ready to go,
I encourage you to use the time you have to let your love show.

In the end, we all must go, and what we leave in our place is as unique as our very own journey,
and hopefully, those left behind won't find our journey unworthy.

Just as your journey began, it will come to an end. At first, you'll feel the journey is slow,
but before you know it, you will start to wonder, "Where did the time go?"

Life is a journey that ends with one last breath on that day, in that moment,
and in one second, you're gone.

When Is It Enough?

When is enough, enough...and how much do we really need?
And why do we think that having more means happiness is guaranteed?

Today, we seem to live in a world that encourages us to have more.
More of this, more of that...more, in fact, than we've ever had before.

Suppose we focused less on 'more' and more on what really makes life worth living?
More on giving thanks, on giving pardon, on giving a hand, on just plain giving.

Suppose having more meant giving more...to those whom most of us try to ignore.
More to the broken and oppressed...to those who may not feel they belong anymore.

Suppose having more meant sharing more...with those whom our giving could restore.
More to those struggling to make a way, to make ends meet...to those who've just never had enough before.

Suppose having more meant owing more...to those whom we would rather stick in a drawer.
More to those who need us to help, rather than overlook... those who are not able to give anymore.

Suppose we asked ourselves how much do we really need?
And if having more really means that we will succeed?

Her Story
(Every woman on a journey has a story to tell)

Every woman has a story as unique as the woman
to whom it belongs.
One that is distinctive, worth hearing, and as rich
and as moving as your favorite songs.

Her story may not be like your story, but it is still
one worth telling.
And if we listen carefully, we might even find it
compelling.

So, let's give her the space and the freedom to tell
it her way.
And we might find within her story...her life, her
pain, and her joy all on display.

As intimate as her deepest secrets and innermost
thoughts is her story.
It will bring you to a level of intimacy so that you
see her in all her glory.

Her story is her history but also a path...to a
freedom that only telling her story can bring.
Not just for her but any who might listen...and hear
her story...without expecting a thing.

Upon Reflection

When you reflect on what you have, you might reflect on the peace that you have...or the pain...or the wisdom that you have that no one can take away. Or maybe the sorrow...or the grief...or the strength...or the time that you have...or the time you no longer have.

When you reflect on what you have given, you might reflect on the love that you have given... the friendships...or the help...or the time you have given that left you feeling energized...or exhausted, the energy you have given that left you feeling elated...or drained. The parts of yourself you have given that can never be returned, or even that which you have given but wish you had not.

When you reflect on what you have received, you might reflect on the love you have received...or the friendships...or that you have received simply by giving. Or the heartache you have received... or the betrayal when you opened yourself up...or the grace you received when you needed it most.

When you reflect on what you have endured,
you might reflect on the loss you have endured...
or the pain...or the trials and tribulations you have
endured. The lessons that you have endured...
or the silence when what you wanted most was
to scream out loud...or the conflict that you have
endured and come out on the other side...maybe
not quite whole, but still alive.

No matter what you reflect upon, I hope that
when you do take the time to reflect and sum it
all up, you find that there is more good than bad,
more love than hate, more satisfaction than regret,
more joy than sadness, more pleasure than pain,
and without a doubt, more memories that make
you smile than memories that make you sigh.

The Fallacy of Time

We have a way of seeing time not as it is but as
we wish it were.
But before we know it, time has passed in what
seems like a blur.

Sometimes, we think there will be time to do all
the things we want to do.
But one day, we realize that somehow, time has
passed us by, too.

When we are young and invincible, time, in all its
glory, seems eternal and endless.
But when we are older and wiser, we realize that
time is something we don't have in excess.

We think we'll have time to tell them how much
we love and appreciate him or her.
But before we declare our love, we find ourselves
wondering how did the unthinkable occur.
How did time get away, and how is it that they
left before our feelings, we could confer?

We think we can tell them tomorrow, that in
looking back, how truly sorry we are.
But before we can tell them, it seems that time
comes up against us like a speeding car.
And all we are left with is sadness, emptiness, and
a gaping scar.

The moral of the story, I guess, is that we can't let
the fallacy of time delay us too long.
Because no one really knows how much time we
have, we shouldn't prolong.
So, let us not let time slip away and leave us
feeling that somehow we got it all wrong.

A Call to Service
(Service and Motherhood)

For me, the call to service came from within.
To serve my country alongside other women and
men.

And with pride and honor, I served without fear.
Wearing my uniform, day after day and year after
year.

Before too long, a tiny someone entered my world.
And while I gave her life, she sent mine into a swirl.

For the first time, my journey truly affected
another.
I asked myself, do I have the strength to be both
Airman and mother?

I looked deep inside, knowing that I could do both.
So, I gathered my strength and readied myself for
unfathomable growth.

I loved serving my country, and the places it took
me.
Figuratively and literally, I knew this was where I
was supposed to be.

Soon, one became three; for my husband and I,
this tripled our joy.
But also the weight of wearing my uniform and
raising two girls and a boy.

My decision to serve, I made without hesitation.
Motherhood, I tackled with the same foundation.

Today, I reflect on my service and am thankful for
the opportunity the Air Force did provide.
I am a veteran and a mother, and I am proud to say
I did both with honor and pride.

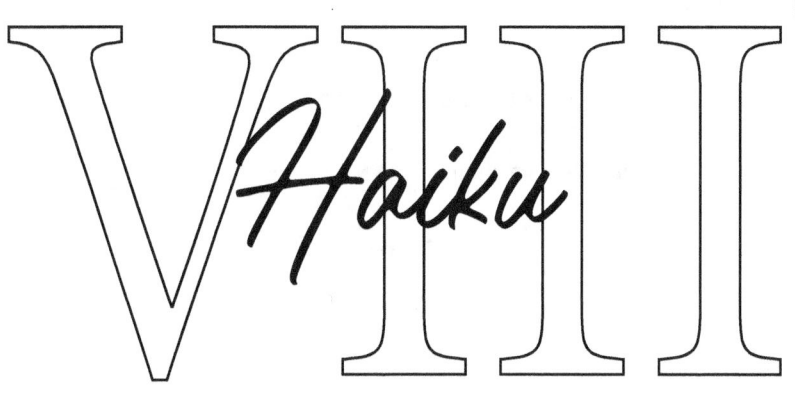

VIII *Haiku*

A traditional Japanese haiku is a three-line poem with seventeen syllables, written in a 5/7/5 syllable count.

"Haiku is not a shriek, a howl, a sigh, or a yawn; rather, it is the deep breath of life."

Santoka Taneda

Haiku #1

The sun shines so bright

The moon shines deep in the night

Time passes too fast

Haiku #2

On the first day, born

On the last, a final breath

Each life a season

Haiku #3

Today, I love you

And tomorrow still, I will

A forever love

Haiku #4

A bird in a nest

A gecko bathed in sunlight

The splendor of life

Haiku #5

Yesterday, a child

Today, in the full of life

Tomorrow, you're gone

Haiku #6

The rain beats down hard

The thunder booms overhead

A song of nature

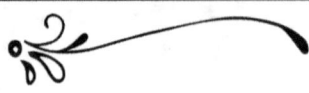

Haiku #7

Buzz of fireflies

Scent of the Honeysuckle

Summer of my youth

Haiku #8

Friends for a short while

My sweet dog, black as the night

Memories for life

Haiku #9

Spring's Cherry Blossoms

Mountains of snow in Winter

Life in Misawa

About the Author

PATRICIA QAIYYIM was born in Michigan City, Indiana. She grew up in a large family and lived in several states throughout the Midwest. After high school, Patricia attended college for two years before joining the United States Air Force.

As a member of the Air Force, Patricia had the opportunity to work in several specialties, and her assignments included bases in Texas, Spain, Arizona, South Carolina, and Japan.

Patricia met her husband while serving in the Air Force, and together, they served more than forty-five years on active duty in the Air Force.

After retirement, Patricia worked as a contractor for several years before deciding to pursue her passion for writing professionally. She published her first book *Moms In The Military Raising A Child While Serving in The Armed Forces* in December 2022, which was awarded the 2023 Military Writers Society of America's Silver Medal. She is currently working on a companion piece to this book.

Besides writing, Patricia is an avid quilter and enjoys all things crafty. She also enjoys reading, cooking, baking, working with her hands, and spending time with her family. Patricia considers herself a woman of faith, a true Renaissance, and a citizen of the world. She believes we should all strive to inspire, motivate, and educate others as we move through life.

Patricia and her husband have three children and two grandchildren.

Published works include:
- *Moms In The Military--Raising A Child While Serving In The Armed Forces*
- *Shrouded In Words: A Collection of Poetry*